MAFIA
MINDED MINISTERS

MAFIA
MINDED MINISTERS
THE STORY OF A MAN'S LIFE IN THEIR MIDST

A Tell All Book By:

NIXON MCDONALD

authorHOUSE®

AuthorHouse™ LLC
1663 Liberty Drive
Bloomington, IN 47403
www.authorhouse.com
Phone: 1-800-839-8640

Published by AuthorHouse 09/05/2014

ISBN: 978-1-4918-6802-7 (sc)
ISBN: 978-1-4918-6803-4 (e)

Library of Congress Control Number: 2014903544

INTRODUCTION

My intentions are not of a negative nature, while thinking over my past experience, I thought I would share some of them with the public. I have held these things in my heart for over forty years. I've decided to share them because there may be someone going through similar things I've gone through; and since I overcame, they may be able to overcome as well.

I was benefitted in many ways, however at the time I didn't see it that way. Hindsight is always twenty- twenty; I can definitely see the benefits now.

God allowed me to come to the Bay Area and accomplish some things that I thought were impossible. I've gone places I thought I'd never go; I've represented on large stages that I never dreamed I would ever stand on.

I have been able to achieve certain things because I had to go through such hard ships; they have made me stronger and more determined.

My prayer is that something in this journal will be beneficial to a young preacher or anyone going through hardships, and they too can overcome!

Mafia in Sicily

Mafia is an attitude of popular hostility to government of any of the groups of Brigands characterized by the attitude. A secret society of criminals thought to exist in the United States and other countries engaging in black mail, illicit trade in narcotics, and other illegal activities.

These are undercover items that, by all means would be taken to keep things from being revealed.

In my early life I enjoyed action packed movies. I especially loved to listen to and watch on black and white television. The Story of Elliot Ness trying to break up illegal activity of selling whisky. Frank Nitti and Al Capone were both the culprits in this film. Elliot Ness would discover one element of their crime, and before you know it, another was taking place.

Anyone that was suspected of exposing them or being a rival to their trade would somehow come up missing. They made sure that their crimes never lead back to the head leader. Never in my wildest dreams would I have thought I'd be the blunt end of the exact same thing. Only instead of the mafia, it was **Mafia Minded Ministers** that had an effect on **another God called minister**.

CHAPTER 1

My Childhood

I was born fifteen miles from a town called Paris, Texas. 10 miles from Paris there was a little stop in the road called Powderly, Texas. It had a service station, a post office and a general store. I lived five miles out in the rural area from that little town.

The roads were dirt except where the white men lived, those were all graveled. There was a settlement called the "McDonald Settlement," that place was called Bradley Hill. There was one way in and one way out. In that settlement there were nine families. I went to school in the church house down from my home. We had only one teacher that taught all grades; however, these were only elementary grades. A lady named Miss Russell was the teacher for a period of time. That same teacher was dating my dad, and one morning my oldest brother went to school a little early and found my dad having sex with her. From that day forward, my dad treated my brother horribly. To me it seemed as if he would have treated him nice, especially since he had such vital information. My brother married at 17 years of age to get away from home. But this same lady fleeced my dad and the whole family out of money, because all of the money that our entire family had earned for the most part was given to Miss Russell.

After attending class in the church house, we had to walk 7 miles to school; and would you believe that same teacher was teaching us along with her daughter who our hard earned money helped go to college. My brother and I walked that seven miles until dad bought us a horse. Every morning after that we rode the horse to school, and one morning we were racing with a car, and the car slowed down at a dip in the road, and the horse ran into the back window of the car. The horse fell down and my brother fell off while I stayed on. Unfortunately, a white boy got cut with the glass from the rear window of the car that we ran into. On our way to school we were saying we had a wreck, but when we got home, my daddy was puffing like a raging bull. We didn't have to get any switches because he already had some. I can remember vividly how, I tried to crawl under the bed, but he pulled me right back out. We received the worst whipping of our lives. To this day my brother and I never have forgotten that whipping. But, we never chased a car again. The schools later consolidated, and all the schools in the area came together and had a teacher for every grade.

When I was a small boy I *had* to go to Church, my mother was a faithful Christian. All of my life I'd never seen or heard her do anything wrong. She was truly a saintly mother. My dad on the other hand wasn't so saintly. He was a deacon in the church, but that was in name only. That is the kind of home I grew up in. My mother insisted on me going to Church every Sunday, and my dad would fuss every Sunday before we would leave going to Church. He would go, but he would always say to my mother, "I'm not going to give that damn preacher my money!" Even then, he was "only giving a dollar" and that he "didn't like the preacher".

When I grew up I didn't like preachers either. I didn't know *why* I didn't like preachers, I just didn't. I guess it was because my dad didn't like them. That was one thing I didn't want to be; a preacher.

CHAPTER 2

Teenager Years

Even though I disliked preachers, I never disrespected them. If my Pastor came through the door of a café where there was a juke-box and I was dancing, I suddenly became a wallflower. We were a poor family. We had to pick cotton. I would pick seventy five dollars' worth of cotton per week, my brother would make one hundred and twenty five dollars a week, my mother would make fifty dollars per week, and my dad would make one hundred and fifty dollars per week. At the end of the week my dad would take all the money, lay it on the bed and count it. Then he would go to the store and get a bag of groceries that you could carry in one arm. Afterwards, he would give me twenty five cents and my brother fifty cents. We would go to the movie which at that time was only ten cent and spend five **cent for popcorn and five cent for a soda. I had five cen**ts left. That was on a Saturday, by Monday my dad was broke.

This kind of behavior happened year after year. He was giving that same school teacher all the money and she was sending her daughter to college. After she graduated college she taught us in elementary school.

My mother would take us to the cotton field near our home where we had to pick scrap cotton which were the leavens after the cotton had been picked the first time. She did this to buy us school clothes. We would get one pair of jeans, one shirt, a pair of shoes and maybe some underclothes. We wore the coat that we had from years before. My brother quit school and got married; but I *had* to remain in school.

By January, those clothes and shoes my mother bought me had holes in them. My jeans had holes in the knees, and had to be patched. By this time the sole of my shoes had separated, and in order to keep them from flopping, I would tie them with wire. There would also be holes in the bottom of my shoes, so I would put cardboard in the shoe but before I would get to the bus my feet would be wet. All of these things caused me to be insecure. I thought everybody was better than I was. When someone would be talking and I couldn't hear them, I assumed they were talking about me. The other children at school went to the lunchroom and I came to school with a bag lunch with a biscuit and syrup in it. I was ashamed to eat around others, so I would go off and eat my biscuit and syrup alone. I was extremely insecure.

I allowed my dad to take my money until I was 17 years of age. One week I started keeping my own figures on the amount of cotton I had picked. When the week end came we gathered around the porch getting ready to collect our earnings. When the man we worked for asked for the figures, I presented mine; he looked at my dad and said, "Nick, what shall I do?" My dad just said "go ahead and give it to him." From that day forward, I received my own money, I was liberated.

CHAPTER 3

High School

Guess what, I made up my mind that I was going to be the best at whatever I did, and I took it out on studying; and as a result, I became the top of my class. I became the captain and top scorer of the basketball team, averaging 28 points a game; I was the highest scorer in scholastic league math competition; I majored in Math and English, was the president of my senior class as well as the Valedictorian. I earned scholarships to 3 colleges, Wiley, Perry View, and Texas Southern. I also promised myself that I was going to wear the best shoes and clothes that they made.

When I graduated and said my Valedictory Speech, I had my bus ticket in my pocket, ready to leave Texas. Unfortunately, I wasn't able to take advantage of the 4 year scholarships in either one of the schools. I had gotten a girl pregnant before I finished school and my parents were very strict. So I did the right thing and married her, but I still continued going to school until I graduated.

My ambition was to be a medical doctor and I could have made it. With a four years scholarship, I could have worked those four years to pay for the next four years, but it didn't happen that way. My graduating teacher counseled me several times, but I had to take care of my wife and my soon to arrive son. I graduated on Friday and left Texas that next day.

CHAPTER 4

ALBUQUERQUE, NEW MEXICO

After leaving Texas I moved to Albuquerque, New Mexico and joined the Macedonia Baptist Church and worked at a service station. I started off washing cars and worked my way up to Assistant Manager.

Not being able to go to college haunted me, so I compromised and went to electronic school. When the class began there were 18 students. By mid-term it had decreased to 9. Another class had decreased to 9 as well, so the two classes joined together. By graduation date, only 9 graduated.

There were many ordeals I had to endure while I was in that class. The class started with three blacks and four Mexicans, the rest were Caucasian. The word "Nigger" was alive and well then; and I had to endure all of those jokes that had the word "nigger" attached. I was alright to a point, however, I didn't appreciate it. When my teacher told a joke concerning race, I was ready to quit. When I left school that night, I didn't intend to go back; but on the way home I said to myself, I'm going to finish this class. And I was the third in my class.

While in Albuquerque I worked as a part time Television Technician until I left town. Electronics did not satisfy my longing for the schooling I had turned down by not accepting one of the 3 scholarships. I sung in a gospel group called the Spiritual Harmonizers for five years in Albuquerque, NM. I was the spokesman of the group and in order to have something to say on a given program, I had to study the bible. I had no idea the result of that move, but after I started studying, strange things started happening to me. When I would get up to emcee the program, I would begin talking and couldn't stop. It was all biblical and it all made sense, but I didn't want that. I didn't want what it suggested, but everyone that I ran into wanted to suggest that I was a preacher.

I had been working at a service station for five years now and had been promised a service station to manage after being the highest salesman in the company of 17 stations, but I kept being denied that position. I was a victim of that invisible ceiling.

My real reason for leaving Albuquerque was to get away from people that were saying that I was going to be a preacher. I had gotten so sick of that. I asked my superintendent if I could have an early vacation. My motive was too leave Albuquerque and go to San Diego, California. I don't know why San Diego, but that is what was in my mind. The superintendent refused to let me go. He said he wanted to give me a service station to manage. Well I had heard that before without him following through with it. I didn't intend on playing that waiting game again.

That was on a Friday afternoon, and on Monday I filled my vehicle with gasoline and left for San Diego. At first my trip was gloomy. I had left my family in Albuquerque, had just a menial amount of money with me and the idea of leaving and going to a place that I'd never been was scary. My relatives tried to persuade me not to go to San Diego because there was no work. But when I asked my dear mother for her advice, she said to me, "Junior, ask the Lord first." That was the only thing that made sense to me, so I did. I prayed a prayer like this: I asked the Lord, "if it is for me to go, make a way, if not, stop me before I go." The very next day I was on the way home from work and people were stopping me on the street asking me to fix their televisions. When I arrived home there were also five televisions in my kitchen to be repaired. When I finished repairing those, I had enough money to leave with my family and enough to take with me on my trip. God can and will make a way!

On my way out of the city limits, I became very depressed. It seemed as if I was in total darkness. Then suddenly, out of nowhere an inspiration came. The Lord revealed to me the scripture, St. John 14th chapter and the first verse which reads, "Let not your heart be troubled ye believe in God, believe also in me." At that moment, the burden left and I had no more burdens all the way to San Diego.

CHAPTER 5

San Diego, California

My friend and I arrived in San Diego, California the next day about 1:00 P.M., and my car generator was making a strange noise. We went to a wrecking yard and I put a used generator on. I picked up a newspaper and there was an ad for a Television Technician at a famous store. The next day I went to that store and filled out an application. The lady told me not to worry, that I had the job.

Notice how God worked, leaving Albuquerque that Monday, this was my off day. We traveled Monday night and arrived Tuesday afternoon and I got the Job on Wednesday morning. I was out of work only one day, at a place where people had told me there were no jobs. I had told a man in Albuquerque before I left, because he said there were no jobs in San Diego as well, you'd better stay here. While I was under the unction of the Holy Spirit I told him that if there was only one job there that I would get that one. God worked it out just that way. The Bible tells us that *"Faith is the substance of things hoped for, the evidence of things not seen."* Hebrews 1:1

WE lived in a hotel when I first arrived in San Diego. After we checked in, a lady said, we will be up to your room soon." I didn't understand the statement. I later realized we had just checked into a hotel that was filled with prostitutes. The lady that came up to our room was loud and was sitting high, exposing herself. I put on a tape of a farewell program that we had before we left Albuquerque. When that gospel tape was heard, she said, "we didn't know that you guys were saved" and left out of the room never to return.

When I acquired a house to live in, I sent for my wife and family. Meanwhile a man that just had preached his first sermon prior to leaving Albuquerque came to San Diego with me. He didn't get a job, so he was living out of my pocket. I rented a house and then my family arrived. You would not believe that this same preacher sent for his family and didn't have a job. He told his wife to sell his car to pay for their ticket, and he didn't have any money other than her fare.

I had two children and a wife he had a wife and four children. They arrived and lived in our house. Whatever food was in the house one particular day was totally consumed. Nothing was left in the house, and my payday was two days off. My wife went to noon day prayer, and one of the mothers of the Church said to her, "Daughter, The Lord told me to take you home with me." When my wife got to her house, she put two empty boxes on the floor in front of the kitchen cabinet and told her to fill them up. She brought home two boxes of food. God supplied our needs. There was no way that woman could have known that we didn't have any food. We had just arrived in the city and just joined the church.

One evening my friend and I discovered this church. He and I were getting haircuts and we heard a gospel program on the radio and asked the barber who it was. He gave us directions on how to get to the church, so we went there and met the pastor that was broadcasting on the radio while we were in the Barber Shop. That Sunday we visited the church and it was dynamite. As soon as our families arrived, we joined.

Upon joining this particular church, I got up to make comments and before I knew it, I was really elaborating on the gospel. My new pastor asked me, "Are you a preacher?" I had come all the way to San Diego to get away from people that thought I was going to be a preacher and now it seems as if I ran right into someone else with those same thoughts. I figured out one thing, you can't get away from God.

I worked in that church for 9 ½ years. During that time, my pastor was totally in my corner. I couldn't do any wrong far as he was concerned. I was the first Brotherhood President, on trial and ordained for Deacon, Co-Chairman of Deacons, Chairman of Trustees, President of Choir, Superintendent of Sunday School, Vice-President of the Cooperation, and Assistant to the Pastor. I worked throughout that entire church. I was trained very well under his tutelage and followed his leadership to the end. I gave out of my own substance to the Pastor's Aid. In fact I was the Pastor's Aid Chairman. I would not talk about him negatively and would not allow anyone else to talk about him. I went on record saying, "I'm not going to hurt him, and I'm not going to let you hurt him." I loved that man as my leader, and totally respected him. He once said to me publicly, when you get ready to go out on your own, I'm going to be with you 100% because you have watched my back, you wouldn't allow anyone to hurt me and I will be with you."

While I was a member of his church and under his tutelage, he gave me some bad advice. I just had finally started preaching and I didn't know anything about preaching, so I was totally dependent on his advice. He told me what I should do when it came to my wife as it related to the gospel. He told me that you can't be too close to your wife because the gospel comes first. Now, I had never been a gospel minister and I was depending on him for everything, including good advice. His bad advice affected my marriage negatively. For example, sometimes I would be studying my lesson for a sermon when my wife would ask me something and it would distract me and cause me to lose my inspiration. Every time that happened I would unconsciously back up from my wife. When I finally came to my senses, I had backed up too far. I tried to put it back together and couldn't. It was too late and we eventually divorced after 24 years of marriage and two sons. Much of that was ignorance on my part because I didn't know how to be a preacher and my wife didn't know how to be a preacher's wife. As a result, I lost a good wife.

While I was a member of the church that he pastored, a young lady was interested in me and I really didn't know what to do with that; I told him about it and he suggested I have sex with her. He said, "You'd better take care of that girl because, if you don't some sinner is going to get her." He gave me the wrong advice again.

Not long after my first message he advised me about my preaching. He told me to "preach deep." He would say to me, "that's it boy, go deep. But as I watched him, I started noticing that he would always preach "shallow." or "simple" and I thought to myself, "this is strange." He wanted me to preach deep so the people didn't understand what I was saying and therefore they wouldn't be hooked on me.

Once again, bad advice! I was even told by him to stop letting the Holy Ghost deal with me while I was presiding over the pulpit, but I told him that I had nothing to do with that. I told him, I'd have to step down because I can't control the Holy Ghost, and neither would I try. You see, I had a lot of respect for the man, and I never disrespected my pastor.

I was later made aware that he told another preacher that if you have someone who has great potential, you lure him over to the edge and when he falls off you will not have to worry about him anymore. I was made aware that I was the one that he planned to lead over the edge.

When I told him that God had commissioned me to start a ministry, he said "that is good." He was the Moderator of the association and he would be the one that would organize any church. The minister that came to San Diego with me also organized a church and my pastor took many of his friends (Pastors) to organize his church. But when he organized our church he would not invite anyone. He organized our church in his office and said to others that the other preacher would be alright but I wouldn't make it six months. From that point on, he fought me with everything he had. For an example, the subject of the first sermon he preached at the church I pastored *was "If you can't run with the footman, how can you run with the horseman?"* From that point, this man systematically tried to dissemble the church I pastored.

The first thing that he was successful in doing was, he paid a lady that was the treasurer of our church to report to him after each service to update him as to the amount of money we received that day.

I found a building to purchase and talked to the owner one morning at 8:00A.M., the owner was going to let the church buy that property with no money down, and at by 5:00 P.M. he had changed his mind and requested ten thousand dollars down. The treasurer had informed my Pastor and he called the owner with some negative information regarding me and the church.

The next thing that happened was this same man (Pastor) put out a rumor that he had to counsel me not to quit preaching. He said that I had a baby by one of the ladies in the church and I was so distraught that I was going to give up preaching. This had never entered my mind. In fact in forty nine (49) years of preaching I've never contemplated quitting, I can't quit. One of his deacons came to me with concerns about me quitting. That is the way I discovered his actions.

This pastor had completely pushed me to anger. So much so, that I wanted to literally kill him. In fact I went to his church office to do just that. I had my gun in my trench coat pocket. When I walked into his office, he was sitting at his desk with his hands in his belt. He talked and talked, never mentioning anything relatively close to the subject at hand. I discovered later that he felt that I came to shoot him. **I AM A WITNESS** that God will certainly warn his servants, and He has no respect of person.

As pastor of a church, I made a grave mistake. I joined the same association and convention that he attended which gave this man the opportunity to build a coalition against me. He was the Moderator of the association and a ranking officer of the State Convention. This man had at least eight pastor's doing his dirty work. Our church was never put on the program to participate in any associational programs, even though we were financially supportive. The only time we were put on program, and it was 150 miles from the city where I pastored. The reason for that was so our members wouldn't be there to support their Pastor; and the coalition that he had formed could freeze me out.

So when I was put on program 150 miles away, I chartered a bus and took 50 members with me. When I got ready to make my opening remarks before I read the scripture and give my subject, one of this Pastor's henchmen sat at the offering table, and taunted me all the way through my message. He said "stop talking and just go ahead and preach." He sat in a position where the audience couldn't hear him but I could. Despite his efforts, he was unsuccessful. God has always brought me out successfully when dealing with His Word. When the service was over, I was entering into one of the local restaurants and overheard a pastor telling my Pastor, "I told you not to put that "Nigger" on program and that he would bring his folk with him."

The next time attempts were made, the association meeting was held at my Pastor's church and as Moderator, he put me on as the principle speaker. On that day, he sent 150 miles to get a speaker and replaced me, even though I was there all the time. And the next time he put the fellow that substituted me on to preach and when the time came, he appointed me to preach at the last minute just to catch me by surprise. His coalition sat down on me in attempts to keep me from looking favorable, but again it failed. They had pushed me in a corner, so much so that I didn't know who I could trust. In fact I couldn't trust anyone. So I had to trust God and He always gave me the victory. The Holy Ghost overshadowed me and totally anointed that service, but that didn't stop or deter them.

When I was away in another city at the association meeting, I was always under watch; even at dinner time I couldn't sit at dinner without being afraid of some attempt to try to get a scandal started on me. I would wait until the entire group of pastors had eaten and gone to their rooms for the night, then I would go and eat my dinner. I was pressured to no end. In Hindsight I don't know how I made it.

The Mafia Minded Minister's method was, they would acquire information from my Pastor and give it to the gossipers of their respective churches and the gossipers would spread it. My Pastor would always keep his hands clean. He would buy you a steak dinner and try to assure you on how much he was your friend. He would say to you, "You know I've never done anything to hurt you," all the while his coalition of ministers was cutting you up with their lies and trickery. He was determined to stop me and my ministry at all cost. At the offset he promised the other preachers that I wouldn't last six months. He must have forgotten that he trained me, and he'd did it well. So when it didn't come to pass the way he wanted, he tried to force it to come to pass.

This man would go to motels with women, and sign my name on the register and be as obvious as possible so people would remember my name. He would go places where crowds of people would gather and drink, chase women and tell them that his name was Rev. Nixon McDonald.

There was a lady that was a member of our church that invited a guest to visit our church. She said "yes." Then the invitee asked who her pastor was, and she answered, "Rev. Nixon McDonald." The invitee immediately replied, "NO, I'm not coming to your church, I wouldn't be caught dead at his church"! My member said, "you don't know my Pastor." The lady said "Yes I'd know him anywhere." She described me as six feet tall and weighing 240 pounds. If I was wringing wet, I'd only weigh 156 pounds. This pastor had used my name and presented himself off as me and in doing so he seriously affected my ministry.

I was invited to one of the pastor's church that was a part of this coalition against me. I was invited to bring the message of that evening, and the pastor sat there in my presence telling nasty jokes while I was getting my mind on the Gospel. If I wanted to step out of the office to keep from hearing them, he would tell me not to go anywhere, sit right there, thus trying to mess up my mind so that the preaching would be diluted.

I served at my Pastor's church for 9 ½ years and was never invited back in that pulpit after I organized a church. Yet, while I was there, I was treated like a king. To get from under the strain of the people asking him to let me preach, he staged an invitation. He heard that I was invited to Rockford, Illinois to conduct a revival, and only then did he put me on to preach on his homecoming program and advertised it on the radio, when he already knew I was going to Rockford. He never asked me to preach, but he told the people that he asked me to preach and I turned it down which took him off the hook of inviting me again.

There was another occasion where this Pastor had gotten into a jam. A woman's husband came to church with a shotgun to shoot the Pastor about having an affair with his wife as well as other incidents.

One day he came to me and said "Mack, you are working too hard. Get in the car."He took me to a hotel downtown, drove his car underground, parked and took the elevator up to the office, paid for two nights and told me to bring my car and park it underground and get some rest. "You look tired" he said. So I did, I called my wife and told her about the nice thing that he had done. I stayed there two days, and when I left the hotel after resting for 2 days, I thanked him for doing such a great thing.

But after I resigned from the church I pastored, I dined with two friends, and I was telling them how rough I had been treated. One of the preachers said, "you haven't had it any harder than I have," but the other preacher said, "yes McDonald has had it very hard," and he began to tell his story. He said, "I was in your Pastor's office when he called all of his associates who were pastor's and said to them, you know all the things that the people are saying about me? It's not me doing those things, it's McDonald." He told the other pastors to get into their cars and let me show you where McDonald is. They were taken down to the hotel that my Pastor had paid for two nights for me to get some rest, and he drove underground and showed them my car. He said "see there, it's McDonald that's doing all those things that I am accused off." At that point I realized that these preachers were indeed Mafia Minded Ministers. The only time I have seen anything like this was in Mafia movies. I never had any idea that a minister of the gospel could do such things.

There was an incident at one of the neighboring churches that our church had a fellowship with, and on that particular night the youth choir was in rehearsal. I had to pick up a couple of youth that didn't have transportation. I picked them up and took them to the church. Afterward, I went to the church that we fellowship with to represent, and because I had the youth rehearsal I would have had to leave early. While all of the Pastors were sitting in the office waiting for the service to begin, I told one of the pastors that I probably would have to leave before the service was over. There were a number of Pastors in the office that I didn't know, and they didn't know me. After I said I might have to leave early, two of my pastor's henchman said "Mac, that is the way you do all the time." One said it and the other agreed by saying "yes you do." I said "no, I've never did that before." He argued, "yes" again and again. Then the "Pastor said "no, no one is leaving!" So I said "well, I'd better give my offering now because I have to go and take some of my youth back home." I left and started back to the church I pastored, then something hit me, I felt totally strange inside, the best way I can describe it, it was as if I had ground up glass in my stomach and my stomach was being rubbed over that glass like a rubbing board. These fellows had pushed me as far as I was going. I took the children home, went by my house, picked up my two guns, and I took my musician home. Suddenly, my daughter grabbed me around the neck and wouldn't let go. I left and I was on my way to kill two preachers that night. I said to myself that three churches would be vacant the next morning. The two preachers churches and the church I pastored. I had gotten to a point that I didn't care. But, because my daughter held my neck so tight, and she didn't know anything about what was going on, I came back to the church and called and asked her mother why she acted that way, because she had never done that before. Her mother said, she said "I don't want anything to happen to daddy." That got my attention, I called a friend and told him what I intended to do and he told me to come and pick him up, and I did. We went out to a restaurant and talked until about 2:00AM. I thought that the feeling was over.

The next morning I got up and the same feeling came over me. I got both of my guns and got in my car and went to one of the preachers houses, but he wasn't there, I went to the place where they drink coffee, they weren't there. I couldn't find them anywhere.

It was two weeks before I would see either one of them again. And when I did, they both met me with a grin. However, by that time, the Lord had taken that feeling away from me. When I think back, God would not allow me to go to that extreme. He also protected those men, which again showed me that God has no respect of person. He warned them. The Devil almost got the victory, but God hindered it. Thank God for Jesus. When you are out of your mind, God is never out of His.

And let me pause and say something that may help somebody that may be going through the same situation. God stopped me through a little girl, but I hope that something that I have written will be able to cause you to go another route. I realized that what I was about to do would have destroyed any chance I had in life totally. God will make up the difference. I am a witness. Thus confirmed by scripture Exodus 14:13 says, *"And Moses said unto the people, fear ye not, stand still and see the salvation of the Lord, which he will show to you today: for the Egyptians whom ye have seen today, ye shall see them again no more forever."*

Two years before I resigned from the church I pastored, I took a lady from our congregation to represent in a musical at the Association that was being held in Blythe, California. She did well because she was a professional singer. During the last half of the program, they honored special requests. People could request their favorite person to sing during that time. I had a burden for six months and I didn't know what it was all about. While sitting there in the church as they continued to call for requests, someone requested for me to sing a solo, but the mistress of ceremony didn't call on me. Someone else asked for me to sing again, however, the program mover still neglected to call me. This happened four times. Finally, the mistress of ceremony said, "we will have the next selection and turn it into the hands of the Moderator." When the person finished singing, a very close friend of mine stood up and said, "we will have a song by Rev. Nixon McDonald." I rose to sing, and sung a verse of "Use Me Lord In Thy Service," and the Lord took me out in a vision and I saw a long shellacked table and I was laying on it with my hands and feet shackled to the table. There were five men holding me down. I saw their faces (all of them are dead now) my pastor and four of his hinchmen. After I left the church and got in my car the burden that I had had for six months left me. I went back to the church that I pastored and resigned. It didn't happen because I thought that I couldn't leave all of the work that I had done. I thought I could fix things. However, in that vision that God allowed me to see, He was telling me to leave. Now in the vision, they were holding me down and would not allow me to move and there was a cord from my navel to the church. For, you see God used me to start the church, and they were holding me, so the church couldn't go anywhere either. So I was supposed to resign, thus cutting the church loose. I just couldn't do it at the time. It took me two additional years and after many other incidents happening. The church attendance started to decrease. I thought I could fix that. The good choir started to disintegrate, everything started going in a negative direction. A female member of the church started attacking as many people in the church as she could find. I preached at a neighboring church one Friday night, and evidently I said something in my message that set her off. She stabbed the tires of every member's car that she could get too that Friday night as well as two of my tires on the same side. She also broke the office window in the church and tried to break the window at my home but the rock hit the ledge instead of the window. Finally, we had to give this member a letter of dismissal from the church. She called and said that if I didn't resend that letter she was going to mess up my reputation. One day after I refused to resend the dismissal letter, I received a call from a friend that said this particular lady called her and asked her to call the police and tell them that I'd raped her and that she would call the Channel 8 News and have them meet the police there. That way it would be all in the news and thus mess up my reputation. She had seen this happen in one of the adjoining cities where a minister had gotten arrested for statutory rape with a 17 year old girl and his name was all over the news. That was the example she used on me, but my friend warned me. However, she didn't give up. One day I was visiting one of the police sub-stations and while I was sitting there, this lady called and tried to convince the captain that I raped her, and the captain said, lady I just don't believe you.

A few days later I received a call from one of the members, that said, did you know that the lady that you dismissed from the church was on the pay-roll of your pastor?" He had paid her to come to our church and get enough negative information on me so that it would become a scandal, and mess up my reputation up, thus messing up the church. I said to myself this is nothing but Mafia Minded mess. It never came to mind that someone in real life could be so dirty, and evil, and especially preachers. I began to look back and recall some of the things that I had encountered, I distinctly remember that same lady trying to get me to accept money from her, she said it like this, Pastor, you don't need to be without money and at that time I was very broke, she said I have four girls on the street, and I will give you $1,350.00 for each girl, per week. You don't have to worry about any money! I will give you money! If, anyone goes to jail, all you would have to do is come and get us out. You would do that anyway, so, no one would know. You wouldn't have to leave your desk. I will deposit the money in your account. Something happened and distracted me, and she left my office without me giving her an answer, and it was about two weeks before I saw her again, and when I saw her, I told her don't think about doing what she had told me two weeks ago. She said again, nobody will know. I told her I know, but I would know, and I'll never do that. The lady just didn't stop, she came to me again with a beautiful Caucasian girl and ask me how do you like her? Then she brought another, and yet another and I asked her why are you bringing these girls for my approval? She said, I thought if you liked her we could go out and have a threesome, or as it is called *ménage-'a-trois.* She tried to get me in a situation that she would have a witness of what I was doing. But, none of these things worked, but it was only by the grace of God. God has a way of making sure you do what He assigns you to do, when God says it, you may as well pack your bags, because God is not going to change His mind.

This process continued with this lady with a scandal0us intent for some time but it didn't work. My Pastor with all of his trickery didn't work either. When God takes over, you can consider yourself on the way. I didn't think of it at the time, but I was almost like Jonah, only I didn't get swallowed up. God took my preaching gift for six weeks, my vocal cords were like loose guitar strings. I would preach and get tired within fifteen minutes, and preaching had never been a problem for me. I thought about going to the doctor, but I realized that it was not a physical problem, it was a spiritual problem. To be totally honest, it actually was a disobedience problem.

Notice the situation that I was in. I was a radio broadcaster for 11 years, and was still obligated to broadcast. I really didn't know what to do, so after five weeks had ended I was probably one of the saddest men around, and on the sixth week, the church had planned to take a bus load of members on a trip to Magic Mountain's recreation park. However, I needed God to move on my behalf. So, I fasted for five days, Monday through Friday.

I ate something on Friday because Saturday I would need my strength. We left San Diego on Saturday morning and we were at Magic Mountain the entire day. I was there in body, but my mind was on my problem. We left the park late that evening, on the way back to San Diego the Lord restored my preaching gift and I was a happy man. Brethren, I used my gift that next day and I told the Lord that I would go where ever He wanted me to go.

Immediately after my promise, I began to go through what seemed like a dark tunnel. It was like I didn't know where I was putting my feet. But I continued to take one step at a time. I would look back and the idea of turning back felt good, but I knew that I couldn't turn back. On September 23rd, 1981, I stepped out the end of that dark tunnel. I was in my office preparing to preach that Sunday morning and my deacon was praying and the people were shouting and praising His name and God cut me loose from that church. I resigned that next Thursday. However, I didn't leave right away. God cut me loose from that church, but He hadn't assigned me to anything. I was just cut loose. I had invited an evangelist to conduct a revival during the week of October 8, 1981 and I hosted him. I didn't preach on Sundays, someone else was taking care of that. Doing the week of the revival, in fact the 8th of October at 1:30 P.M. God commissioned me to Oakland, California and to the Mt. Tabor Baptist Church. I didn't want any part of that, but me being upset didn't change anything. My car wasn't fit to drive, so I pulled the engine out of my car and rebuilt it myself and put it back in and got my car ready for the road. The church gave me a going away party on the 6th of December 1981. They gave me suits and other gifts, and some money. During this time, my son acknowledged his call to the gospel ministry and I was compelled to stay in

San Diego to hear his first message, which was on the 31st day of January 1982. He did very well and I listened to his second message on that next Sunday. I left San Diego on the 8th of February 1982 and headed to a place that I had never been before.

CHAPTER 6

FINALLY LEAVING SAN DIEGO

February 8th, 1982 @ about 7:00 A.M., I left San Diego, California and the only thing I knew was that God directed me to Oakland, California. I'd never been to Oakland, I didn't know anyone in Oakland and I didn't even know how far Oakland was from San Diego. But when you've gone through as much as I had at that point, it didn't matter because I had promised God that where ever He wanted me to go, I would go. Actually, I hadn't gotten any further than Magic Mountain on highway Interstate-5. I had heard about the Grape Vine, but had never been there before. That travel was the most lonesome travel that I've ever traveled. As I was going through the Grape Vine, God showed me two Old Testament characters, Abraham and Job. Well I realized what the character Abraham meant, but it didn't dawn on me what Job meant.

Arrived in Oakland

I arrived in Oakland, to my surprise at 5:00 P.M. the same day I left San Diego and didn't know where to go. I didn't know where to ask anyone where to go. I got off the freeway on a street called Seminary and flagged a policeman down and asked him where a good motel was and he told me where the Six Pence Inn was. I got lost and ended up on Seventh Street downtown Oakland. I rented a room in this raggedy motel and after shutting the door, you could still see outside through the cracks in the door. I put as much of the furniture across the door as I could move against the door, and slept with my 38 revolver in my hand. The next morning I received some instructions on how to get to The Six Pence Inn. When I arrived there I paid for a week. It started raining and it rained for two weeks. It rained so much that the ground couldn't absorb the water.

Since God had commissioned me and gave me the name of the city and the church, the first thing I did was look in the city phone book looking for the Mt. Tabor Baptist Church, of which there was none. I thought that since God directed me here and gave me the Church name it would be a church here that was named Mt. Tabor, but I was wrong.

Now since I'm not pastoring, I've got to find a job and that is something I hadn't done for some time. However, I was equipped with the knowledge of electronics, so I headed to Silicon Valley where all of the electronic plants were located. When I arrived there, I got the news that there was a six month freeze on hiring, I ended up in a traffic jam and I thought I'd never get back to the motel. I got out of my car on the pavement and the water came up over my shoes. It was raining so much I could hardly see. I thought to myself, what have I gotten myself into. In a strange land, around strange people, and on top of that, it's not going to stop raining and the people wouldn't even speak.

Here I am all the way in Northern California on two words from the Lord, Oakland and Mt. Tabor. I had a sister that lived in Richmond California. I thought Richmond was a 100 miles from where I was. I called her and she began to fuss at me about why didn't I come to her house and I told her I didn't know that she lived in the area. She told me to leave the motel and come to her house but I couldn't get my money back so I had to stay through the week that I paid for. I visited my sister after she gave me directions to her house, and you wouldn't believe that she lived only 22 miles from where I was in the motel. She said to me, you are going to live at your niece's house and you are going to eat here and it's not going to cost you anything. Well, it seemed like things were looking up, and it was a good thing because I didn't have much money. I looked for a job from the length and breadth of the Bay Area with no success. I was driving a 1970 Lincoln Continental Town Car, and it could pass everything on the highway except the service station. I would fill it up in the morning and by the time I got home it was half empty. It had a 29 gallon tank, so looking for a job got very expensive.

One day I thought I was almost at the bottom of my life, I was very distraught, I said to the Lord, "take me to the bottom fast. The next day I was driving down Mac Arthur Boulevard in Oakland, California and I saw a man sitting in a doorway with a blanket around him, and he was shivering. I said to the Lord please don't take me to the bottom. I wasn't anywhere near the bottom. I lived in a four bedroom house, with central heating, television, phone and everything I needed, I was nowhere near the bottom.

I looked for a job for one month and couldn't find one, and one day my sister was talking to my cousin who lived in Vallejo, California and she mentioned that I was a Television Technician. My cousin's husband overheard the conservation and when she got off the phone he asked her who was she talking too and she said Julia my sister, and he said call her back because I know someone that is looking for a Television Technician. She called my sister back and said my husband knows someone that needs a T.V. man. The arrangement was made without my help. They arranged for me to meet the man one Saturday at 4:00P.M., and I met him. When this man got out of his truck, he was smiling and said when God blesses you like this it's hard to believe. He said he was trying to work at the television shop and also get his retirement from Mare Island and he needed someone to take care of the shop. His shop was full of televisions stacked up to the ceiling. We talked a while and he gave me the keys to his shop, and told me I could come when I wanted too and leave when I wanted too. I worked there for exactly one year and totally cleared his shop out with un-repaired televisions. Before I finished working there I moved from my niece's home to Vallejo, California to a small hotel on Virginia Street and stayed there for about 6 months.

While I was at that hotel, the commission was still in my mind. But I was getting discouraged. I was working in Vallejo, about 34 miles from Oakland, and God specifically said Mt. Tabor and Oakland, and I hadn't heard from God at all since October 1981. It's about June of 1982, and I'm working 34 miles away from the place I am supposed to be.

One night I got so restless and discouraged I could not sleep. I left my hotel room and went to a restaurant and ordered some coffee. I sat there until about 1:00 A.M., and still no consolation. I went back to my room and sat there about another hour, and the Lord revealed to me, **LO I AM WITH YOU ALWAYS EVEN UNTIL THE END OF THE WORLD**, that lifted me up, and I got up out of the bed and praised the Lord the Rest of the night. The load that I was carrying was lifted, and a new determination was kindled in me and I was ready to tackle anything.

But, what I didn't understand was that I just may have to tackle anything. I sent for my family and didn't have anywhere for them to stay, so we stayed in the hotel room for about a month and had to move soon because of hotel regulations and we wouldn't have anywhere to stay. We searched the newspapers, found an apartment in Oakland. We didn't have the money with us to pay for the apartment, and the manager wouldn't allow us to put a down payment on it to hold it. But, my wife said to the manager, can we give you half of the money and go get the other half and bring it back today?" The apartment manager said yes. So we did.

We moved in that week-end because they wanted us out of the hotel. The manager of the apartment said the carpet was wet, but we moved in anyway. We didn't have any furniture. We put our clothes on the floor and made a sleeping place for my wife, me and our daughter, because our furniture was in storage in another City. I was still working 34 miles away, 68 miles around trip, and I traveled those miles every day, 5 days per week for 7 months and then I quit my job because God had commissioned me to Oakland and I was in Vallejo all day and it didn't leave any time to try looking for a place to establish a church to be obedient to the Lord. I had a car payment of $210.00 per month, rent was $350.00 and the gasoline that it took to travel, food, utilities, etc., And I quit my job! Let me tell you, you can make it if you depend upon God, if God sent you He will provide for you. I was a Television Tech by trade and I went to St. Vincent DePaul and purchased used televisions and repaired them and put ads in the news-paper, 7 days for $7.00. I would also repair as many televisions as I could and put them in the back room. When someone would call and purchase a television, I would put another out until all of them were gone. Sometimes it would be the same day our PG&E, Telephone and/or rent was due. We would be able to satisfy all of our bills. God allowed it to happen over and over again.

I was offered a job at Naval Air as an Electronic Tech, but the Lord would not allow me to take it. At the time I had more electronic education than anyone in the plant. But I couldn't take it. I badly needed the money, but I couldn't take it. The apartment complex was a gated community. There was a security gate to enter. However, I didn't know why, because it seemed as though all of the rebel rousers were already inside. They played music all night every night. I can understand the woes of Lot in Sodom, because he didn't have a testimony because he was vexed with filthy conservation. The same things applied to me, I couldn't witness to anyone there because, when I arrived home from work, as soon as I turned into the complex I would get angry because I knew that I was going to be bombarded with loud music all night.

When I went to work I was traumatized, however to some degree I was free from the torture of the music until evening. That anguish went on for about a year. I was still on my search for a place to start a church. I would ask about a place and they would give me some outlandish price that I couldn't afford and I was so discouraged. Instead of asking for a building for a church, I started asking for a building for television service. Then I made up some flyers and passed them out for television service, and not far from where I lived a lady called me for television service. I went there and we sat there on the couch and I talked. And I discovered that I had just found a Christian. I told her about what I was trying to do and she said I have a romper room down stairs that will hold about 90 people, you can use it to start a bible class. We started a bible class there and she was a part of the class. It was going good. However, I still needed a building for the church. The character of Oakland is such that the people would not speak. They would look you in the face and wouldn't speak. I asked the Lord, how can I build a church and the people won't even speak? Listen, I didn't understand the trials and suffering that I would have to go through in leaving one city and going to another to establish a church. I soon found out that the characters that I saw coming over the Grape Vine had meaning. Abraham was about faith, but Job was about suffering, and I didn't get the gist of it until now. I had to face much suffering. In order to understand the character of Oakland, I had to sit in the trenches and observe Oakland's people. These folks would look you right in the eye and would not speak! So, I watched them for a while, and when they are approaching you they will not speak, but when they get right even with you, they will cut their eyes over at you, and then they will speak. I had to learn these folks before I could witness to them. I believe every city has its own characteristic and in order to be effective, you must learn these traits. I didn't realize that Oakland was the headquarters of the Black Panthers, and when the leader were arrested, the others fled into the hills. But when they came down they had a hard core and an attitude to go with it. They also seemed to have to prove how tough they were.

Prior to finding a place, I had asked some people to be a part of the church. I had commitment cards, 32 people to start the church. I then proceeded to find a place to have our worship service. I went to the School Board and they gave me a contract for 13 weeks to the auditorium of the King Estate, Jr. High School and it was $ 96.00 per week. The Lord burdened me concerning the church, and I called a meeting the Tuesday night before the Sunday that we were supposed to have our first worship service and no one showed up. I almost fell in a trap that the Devil had set, but God warned me in time. Thus a confirmation of Scripture, Except the Lord keep the city, the watchman watch, but in vain." I went back to the school board and asked them to cancel the contract and they did. God worked on my behalf and I gave Him praise. One day, as I returned home from looking for a place for a church, (actually I had stop asking for a place for the church and started asking for a place for a television service, because people were turning their nose down on the idea of a church). I arrived to my home and my wife said, there was a man who called about a place. I was so tired of hearing the word no, that I started not to call back, but I did, and the first thing the man said to me was "are you a born again believer," and I said yes. That sounded strange to me after all of the negatives that I had encountered. He ask me to meet him at the place and when I met him, we sat down on two five gallon cans and talked about the building for about 10 minutes and proceeded to talk about Jesus Christ for about two hours. When I got ready to leave he gave me the keys to the building and also gave me the lumber to build the platform needed.

No money exchanged hands. This man was very helpful to Mt. Tabor Baptist Church. We acquired the building in June of that year while we were still having Bible Class in the lady's romper-room. We did so until the platform and signs were finished. I didn't know hardly anyone in the city. However, when we got ready to start the church, we had gathered Sister Loretta Kyle, her daughter Carla Gaines, my wife Sister Louise McDonald, our daughter Thedra McDonald, Mrs. Wheeler and we borrowed two members from Trinity Baptist Church, and Rev. E. Calvin from Vallejo, California. We started having worship on the 3rd day of July 1983 and we organized as a church on July 13th. We had 5 people and we borrowed 3 and Rev. J. W. Morrison moderated the meeting. Rev. Leroy Holland, Sr., Rev. Williams, Rev. E. Calvin and Rev. O. Bernstein were the counsel that organized the Mt. Tabor Baptist Church, all of which have passed away, except for Rev. E. Calvin.

Our first offering was $121.00 and we only had 4 members present and two guests, it was tough at first because we had no means of advertisement. I had been accustomed to being on the radio, but the only thing we had was our mouth. A young man would be passing by the church while the platform was being built and say, oh you trying to build a church. Then he would say some negative things and would connect some other choice words with it. Within two month time, the same man came to me for counseling. God always backs up His word. Whatever He promised He will keep. A young man that I was to fix televisions for gave me a television shop on East 14th Street. I was doing contract work for him because he didn't know how to repair TV's or run a business. This young man signed this business over to me and I thought that God was getting ready to give me back my businesses that I had to close by leaving San Diego, but to my surprise as soon as I was the Owner, it seems as if an invisible hand was placed over the door. The same people that came in frequently stopped coming in at all and I was the one that was running the place before it was signed over to me. I believe that God was saying to me, no to television service, in that He sent me here to build a Church. He would not allow the TV business to progress. The same man that allowed me to get the building for the church came back and asked me why don't you move your living quarters upstairs. He had an apartment two doors from the church building. I said no. He said here are the keys, and if you decide to, you can move in. After looking at the place I moved in that evening.

Two weeks later, this same man came back and asked me, how much are you paying for rent per month for the your TV shop? I said $ 250.00, he said that is too much. Why don't you move in next door? I will put bars on the windows and he did. I moved in that place and now I have three buildings that belong to him. He came back the first of the month and waived all of the rent on all three places. Now, I've been holding this testimony for a long time, now it's time to tell all. Not only did he waive the rent, he came once pre month and wrote out a check for $100.00 dollars and gave it to the church. What I'm trying to say is that no one can stop what God has ordained.

Now after moving into this place, a good location, God had other plans for me. I thought maybe this is it, the big break, but no. I put video games in the place, I put candy and other snacks in the shop, but the children would go five blocks down the street to play video games and pass right by my candy and snacks. God means just what he says. I can recall the words that God revealed to me back in San

Diego. Mt. Tabor and Oakland. God intended for me to build a church in Oakland and not a TV shop.

Can I give you a praise report? Soon after we started the church someone put an envelope in the mail box, green in color and had writing on it in black marker pen and I looked in it and there was $ 376.00. I still don't know to this day where it came from. Not long after that someone put a cashier's check for $500.00 dollars in the box made out to the Mt. Tabor Baptist Church and I never found out who brought it, but I really do know who sent it, it had to be God. God worked in our behalf over and over again. *Someone told a story about a lady that didn't have any food, and began to pray that God would send her some food. This young man over heard her praying and thought he would work a prank on her. He went through the neighborhood and collected food until he had collected two boxes and came and placed the boxes of groceries at her door and ring the doorbell and ran. The lady came to the door and seen the groceries and said, "Thank you Jesus," and the boy jumps out from behind the bushes and said, see there, it wasn't Jesus it was me: The woman replied, the Devil may have brought it, but Jesus sent it.*

When money got low I would crave for a job, and sometimes I would get a job. But as soon as I did, it would turn out to be nothing. When I would get a job and it didn't work out and I had to start back solely depending on God by faith, the faith that I had accumulated by God making a way had now vanished, because now I'm depending on the job and not completely on God. Now I had to rebuild my faith and it seems to be harder the second or third time than it was the first time.

I made a statement to my wife, I'm not going to fail God anymore, which was in April, and I done alright for a year, it was April again and I had only one dime in my pocket. I felt distraught, I was sitting in my office on a choir rehearsal night, and a member came through the door and said, I see you squinting, get some glasses with your money and you need a top coat, and the rest of the money is yours. She gave me an envelope, and left out of my office. I looked into the envelope and there were **ten one hundred bills** in there. I guess you know, I could hardly contain myself. Then I thought, this woman is trying to buy me, so I called her the next day and asked her, what was all that money about? And she said you will have to ask God, because I couldn't rest until I went to the bank and withdrew the money. The only thing I could say is thank God, and I am truly a witness that God will provide. Notice the things that I accomplished in San Diego was done with finances and the things I have accomplished in Oakland have been by faith.

God is a Marvelous God and He is not that just on Sundays, He is God 24-7! If you are depending on God for what he can do at church, let me tell you, you can depend upon God in every area of your life, and I'm a witness to that.

Notice here that because of my past experience, I was leery of preachers to the point that I didn't trust them at all. And when someone has done something close to what I had been through, I was ready to retaliate. I was equipped to do so, because I had earned my Black Belt in Karate and I had experience in professional Boxing, as well as being a marksman with a fire arm. I had sworn to myself that I wouldn't allow anyone else to take me through what I had been through ever again, even if it meant my life or life in prison. I hope you can see the impact The Mafia Minded Minister's had on me. I was determined to hold fast to what I had said. In order for you to understand what I'm talking about, there was an incident in one of the minister's union where one fellow took the liberty of calling me Richard Nixon. Let me tell you of a few incidents that happened to me while I was in San Diego. In President Nixon's era they used my name as a joke. My dad was also named Nixon and he named me Nixon McDonald, Jr., and that was a long time before I had heard of Richard Nixon. Everyone's reputation is built on his or her name. So they took the liberty of making a joke out of my name. Now that I am in a new city trying to make a good reputation for myself, what the fellow didn't understand was that I had been through all kinds of humiliation for a long time and was not about to let it happen again. Even when I would be introduced to preach, some of the Mafia Minded Ministers would make a joke out of my name, even on the floor of the District Association. I was very tired of being the blunt end of a people's jokes. I told the preacher of the Minister's Union in the Bay Area several times not to make a joke out of my name. But because I build my reputation on my name, in a new town and I need a good reputation so don't mess it up. But he ignored it, and one day at the Minister's Union as he was taking the dues, he was about to do what I had asked him not to do and at that particular time I was prepared to break his neck with a Karate Chop, and evidently he sensed it, and from that day forward he never did that again.

It's not good to take the liberty to do or say things to people, that you don't know, because you don't know who they are or what they have been through and it can cause an adverse effect on the person and also on you.

Doing the time of all of the negatives, I had to be very careful not to become bitter under circumstances of this nature. When I first arrived in the Bay Area, I would stand off from preachers, I would speak, but I wouldn't have any interaction with them because I didn't trust them.

Let me tell you how all of this started. While I was around the Mafia Minded Ministers, I was treated so badly, not just by the preachers, but they had gotten their members involved in this conspiracy. When I was at the Association I was segregated against other preachers, so much so that I had to go alone, and finally I started feeling good about being alone. I started enjoying myself. I had a smile once, but in time I lost my smile. That is why I stood alone when I arrived in the Bay Area and maintained it for a long time. Brethren I discovered something, all ministers are not Mafia Minded. It took me a while to get the stench of San Diego's Mafia Minded Minister's off me. But thank God I did. I have to admit to you that before I got it all together, I was very sensitive toward preachers. I didn't trust them at all. I had a few incidents where, if a preacher got close to doing the things that I had been through, I got them off me real quick. I would not allow any preacher to get close to me and I wouldn't get close to them. I stood off from them for a long time. I realized the things that you go through can very easily become a part of you and your demeanor.

Nixon McDonald

A Different Outlook

When I arrived in the Bay Area I united with the Providence Baptist Church of Richmond California, Pastored by the late Dr. Elijah Brocks. This was a great man, however, I was leery of him for a while also, and I looked at every preacher with suspicion. But Dr. Brocks was very good to me. Actually I didn't think preachers could be nice. Being in the Bay Area started to change me a little. However, I ran into some duds here also, but for the most part this was a different set of preachers.

While I was a member under the late Dr. Brocks, I couldn't have asked for better treatment. If he knew I was struggling, he would try to open a door for me. If he thought I was going at something the wrong way, he would caution me about it.

This Pastor let me do two revivals at Providence Baptist Church and treated me as if, I was a guest from out of town. I was treated very well financially and I was just a member there. Brethren, I was literally blown away. I had never been treated like that by my Pastor before. From that point, I started looking at preachers a little different. However, I still had doubt. Through this man I started meeting pastors in the area and they started treating me the way I should have been treated all along. I joined one of the local Associations and was treated well there. When I started pastoring I met a lots of good ministers. Of course I have a little better prospective now, and I realize that in any field there are some good and there are some bad. So, it gives you the ability to eat the meat and throw the bone away. Now I still hadn't opened myself to everyone. I joined a Minister's Union and thought that for the most part that I was being isolated. However, that was just leftovers thoughts from San Diego. Because when I started watching them closely, it was me that didn't open up to them. When I did open up, I found out that these were the nicest guys that anyone could be around. I then started looking forward to being with them every Tuesday. Now, I needed a new Pastor since Dr. Brocks had passed away. I looked and looked. There were three Pastors in the area that I was looking at. I scrutinized them to no end. However, they didn't know it. I reduced it down to one and his name is Dr. Joe L. Smith, the Pastor of the Good Hope Baptist Church of Oakland, California. He is a solid man. He is a strict man and he is a man that can and will stand on his word. I went to his 8:00A.M. service one morning after watching him for one year and when I got out of my car he said, "I don't feel well, bring something with you, I want you to preach for Me." I preached that morning and then joined his church and he has treated me great as a man, as a member, and also as a preacher. I feel very comfortable around him, and the Good Hope Baptist Church.

Out of all of the things that I had been through, God was sill blessing the ministry. God allowed us to purchase a building after being at the same location for a period of eleven years. Some of the pastors around town, said to me you need to get a place. They said they liked to see a church progress. They meant well, but I understood what was going on in the back room. It would be dangerous to allow someone on the outside to dictate what you do on the inside. The pastor didn't know that I had almost as much experience as he had, but I didn't say anything out of the way to him. When God got ready, someone put a flyer in our mail box, offering us a building for $130,000.00. The building was 5,000 square feet. Three other parties were interested in the building. Would you believe that the owner would not sell to the other interested parties. He proceeded to sell it to us.

We tried to get it financed, but that didn't work. The seller said that's okay, give me $21,000.00 down and we will carry the rest. We only had $10,000.00 and we needed $11,000.00 in one month and we normally couldn't get that much money in eleven years. I told the members about it, and they said yes. Two weeks later I said we need to start giving the money, and within five minutes I had $5,500.00 in my hand. In twenty one days I had all of the money. Some of the members would give me $ 500.00 at a time and some would give me $1,000.00 at a time. I wanted to show you how God worked things out for me and the Mt. Tabor Baptist Church that He sent me to establish.

I joined the Progressive District Association and was accepted there. Not long after that I joined the Southern Baptist Association, Named East Bay Baptist Association where I worked in many areas and traveled many places over the nation. I was the liaison to the black churches. I was the Vice moderator for two years and also was elected as Moderator. At that time I was sought out to organize an Association out of the Western Baptist Convention. After much deliberation I accepted the challenge and organized the association in March 1996. At a time I was still the Moderator of East Bay Baptist Association. I was moderator for two associations at the same time. However there was no conflict. The new association grew to about seventeen churches and there came a conflict in management of the convention. All of the churches removed themselves from the Western Baptist Convention and joined the California State Baptist Convention and was successful. Our unity was second to none with the

California State Baptist Convention. In the fifth year of our Association, I was elected the chairman of Moderators of the California State Baptist Convention and served for five years. I served as Moderator of the Tri-Valley District Association for a period of 10 years and East Bay Baptist for two years. God has allowed me to pastor the Mt. Tabor Baptist Church of Oakland California, Inc., for 31 years, the same church that He sent me to establish.

I am a member of the Bay Cities Minister's Union and I've never enjoyed ministers like I enjoy these fellows and the brother's here respect each other. My Pastor is the President of the Union and he says what he means and means what he says and stands on it. I've learned what it means when it says, "*how good and how pleasant it is for brethren to dwell together in unity.*" I have been privileged to preach in Conventions, Associations, huge banquets and many revivals. God has opened many doors for me and He has allowed me to still preach strong I am 77 years of age and my preaching seems to get stronger instead of weaker. I'm much like Caleb, I feel stronger now than I did before I left San Diego. My Pastor, Joe L. Smith called me one day while I was getting a physical and he asked me to preach on his conferring service and I told him, I appreciate the offer, but I have my Deacon and Deaconess Annual Day and Dr. George Epps is my guest speaker and I can't come. The very next day I was at the same place getting the results of my test and God gave me a message about the conferring service and I was preaching it in my Pastor's pulpit. I called my Pastor back and the call went straight to voice mail. I tried over and over again until finally after an hour I reached him. I asked him did you fill that spot and he said no, I told him you've got it filled now.

Now the service was great. In fact, that was the greatest privilege that I have ever had. I've had greater numbers, but this occasion was off the hook, if I may say that! The preachers just kept coming in. Not just preachers, those with their Doctorate degrees, all of those hooded doctor robes. I would have missed the highlight of my life, if I had not been there. This was a hooding ceremony for my Pastor, Dr. Joe L. Smith. I had doctors all around me and God so fixed it that I had to bring the message and He blessed that service. Hats off to Dr. Joe L. Smith and many thanks to him for allowing me to stand in that spot. I am very grateful for this man. Things like this tend to make you forget all about of the Mafia Minded Ministers of the past. When things happen in a negative way, God is setting you up for a blessing.

Closing

In closing this writing, I would like to conclude by saying when you can look over your life and see where the Lord has brought you from, you can say, thank the Lord. When you have been through what the Psalmist indicated when he said, thou my enemies came upon me to eat of my flesh, they stumbled and fell, the Scripture enlarges itself within you and you can't keep from praising the Lord.

When God has pulled you out of the claws of the lion and the hugs of the bear, you don't have to guess whether God can deliver or not, you know that He can. After God has allowed all of this to come upon you, and you can come out more than a conqueror you know God is real. When you've been through bitter anguish, and come out a happy man, you can say thank God because you are better than I was before I started.

Thank God for my immediate family that has been a blessing to me. I can truthfully say, I am happier than I've ever been in my life. I love my Wife, I love my children, grandchildren and also my great grandchildren.

I feel that because of what I've been through, I was a preacher when I started, but without a doubt, I am a better preacher now. It's a good feeling to be able to stand in the midst of some of the greatest, and yet God still makes you look great. It's good to be able to stand in the gospel circle and easily proclaim the unsearchable riches of the Gospel of peace and see the results.

The only thing I can say is, I couldn't have made it without God. When I was about to crumble, He put me back together again. When I was about to explode and ruin my life and my family's lives, God spoke peace to my soul. All I am and all I hope to be, I owe it all to God.

Readers of this book, when you run into Mafia Minded Ministers, remember to, hold on to God's hand and no one can overwhelm you, God is stronger than they are. Don't let anyone rob you of your blessing, because God has a blessing special for you. Everybody has an hour, everybody has a spotlight, nobody can take your hour or spotlight. While God is allowing others to work on you, you be sure to be working on yourself. God allows us to go through things to strengthen us for the journey ahead. Only you can determine your destiny, only you can shatter your own dreams, stand when it seems impossible to stand, and when God gives you victory, don't forget to give Him the glory.

Some Men that have had an influence on my ministry in the Bay Area

(Some are living and some have gone onto meet the Lord):

The Late Dr. Elijah Brocks, The late Dr. J. W. Morrison, The Late Brother Meade Jackson, Dr. T. P. Fields, Dr. Albert Nichols of Los Angeles, and last but not least Dr. Joe L. Smith. Let me also thank my wife, Mrs. Louise McDonald, my daughters Nikija Chandler and Thedra Allen, they have been a great inspiration to me.

I also want to thank my son, Rev. Dwight McDonald, Sr. and Rev. Dwight McDonald, Jr., because when I was sick, my wife, daughters, son, and my grandson were right there. I also thank the members of the Mt. Tabor Baptist Church that I've been privileged to organize and pastor for thirty one 31 years. I love you, I love you, I love you. I've dedicated my life to you and I also dedicate this book to you.

Dr. Nixon McDonald

About the Author

Dr. Nixon McDonald
The Biography

Dr. Nixon McDonald, Jr., was born to Nixon McDonald, Sr., & Rosa McDonald on May 1, 1937 in Powderly Texas. He attended the Powderly High School where he earned the award of being all-around gentleman of the school. He majored in Math and English, scored the highest mark in the Scholastic Math Competition in the District, played basketball, was the highest scorer of the team, and was also the captain of the team. He also ran track & field. He was also the valedictorian of his graduation class; he won a four –year scholarship. From there, he moved to Albuquerque, New Mexico where he sung in a gospel group for a total of for a total of five (5) years. He then moved to San Diego, California and joined a Baptist Church and served in many capacities in the church. After four years he accepted his call to the Gospel

Ministry, and served as the Assistant to the Pastor for six years.

He organized a Baptist Church in 1970 and pastored it for a period of 11 years, while broadcasting on AM and FM Radio. He moved to Oakland, California in 1982, and organized the Mt. Tabor Baptist Church and Remains the Senior Pastor thirty one (31) years. He holds a Bachelors, Masters and two Doctorate Degrees. He reached this plateau so would be able to make the word understandable to the listeners.

Dr. McDonald has pastored a total of 42 years and has been preaching for 50 years, he is a dynamic Preacher, Teacher, Counselor, and Evangelist. Dr. McDonald held the office of Moderator of the East Bay Baptist Association of the Southern Baptist Convention; he also held the office of Moderator of the Tri-Valley Missionary District Association, and the chairman of Moderators of the California State Baptist Convention.

He is also a family man, married with children, grandchildren and great grand- children.